I0823254

Nature's Rivals

Mongoose vs. Cobra

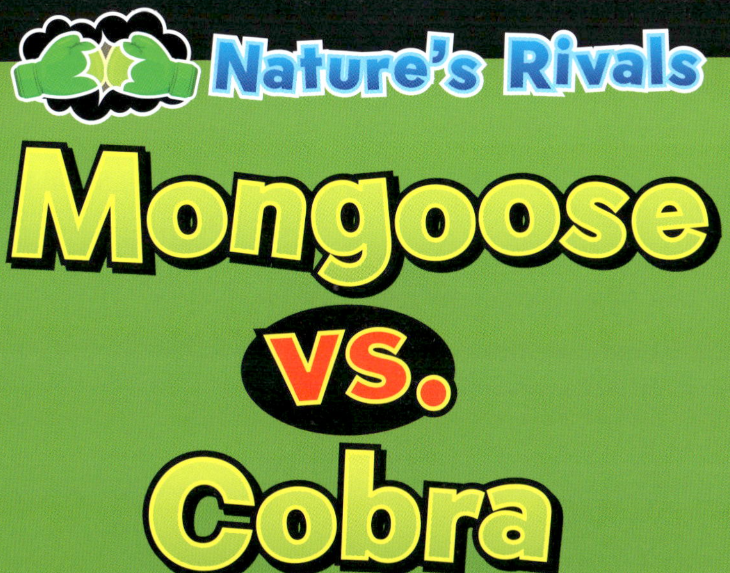

JOANNE MATTERN

Mitchell Lane
PUBLISHERS

Parent and Caregiver Tips for Creating Nonfiction Readers

The high-interest topics in the *Nature's Rivals* series are sure to get your young reader excited about reading nonfiction. While exploring a fascinating subject, your reader will be introduced to new concepts, facts, ideas, and vocabulary.

Tips for Reading Nonfiction

Talk about Nonfiction

Explain that nonfiction books provide facts about real-world topics. When readers read nonfiction, they gain a rich understanding of the world. They build background knowledge that provides a foundation for learning and academic success.

Look at the Parts

This book contains the following helpful features. Share the purpose of each feature with your reader.

Photos, Captions, and Graphic Aids
The photos, captions, charts, maps, and other graphic aids in nonfiction texts contain a wealth of information. Help your reader identify different ways information can be displayed.

Sidebars
These extra tidbits of information help satisfy readers' curiosity and expand their knowledge.

Table of Contents
Located at the front of the book, this list shows the big ideas within the text and the page numbers where they can be found.

Glossary
Located at the back of the book, the glossary defines key words and phrases that are related to the topic. These words and phrases can be found in the text in **bold** type.

Comprehension Questions (Fact Check)
Multiple-choice questions help readers self-check to make sure they understand what they read.

Index
Located at the back of the book, the index is an alphabetical list of topics and the page numbers where they can be found.

With a little help and guidance, your reader will be on their way to enjoying and learning from nonfiction books.

Mitchell Lane
PUBLISHERS
mitchelllanepub.com

2001 SW 31st Avenue
Hallandale, FL 33009

First Edition, 2026.
Author: Joanne Mattern
Designer: Jen Bowers
Editor: Tricia Hoffman

Series: Nature's Rivals
Title: Mongoose vs. Cobra / by Joanne Mattern

Hallandale, FL : Mitchell Lane Publishers, [2026]

Library bound ISBN: 979-8-89260-604-2
Paperback ISBN: 979-8-89260-616-5
eBook ISBN: 979-8-89260-605-9

PHOTO CREDITS
Shutterstock: Kurit afshen, cover and 1, 2, 7, 17, 18, 26, 27; dwi putra stock, 4; BlueBarronPhoto, 4; Lauren Suryanata, 5, 28; Ilia Krivoruk, 6; thsulemani, 8; MIKOPhotography, 9, Thomas Torget, 9, 28; dodafoto, 10; Photography Phor Phun, 11, R J Endall Photographer, 11; Elen Marlen, 12; Danita Delimont, 13; Isroi, 14; Wildsight, 15; Pornchaiwalyakarn, 16; Padodo, 19; Yash2109, 20; Ton Bangkeaw, 21; Riadi Pracipta66, 22, 23, 25; Cavan-Images, 24; Andrei Minsk, 28

Contents

Dangerous Prey

A mongoose slips through the long grass. He is hungry and looking for food. This small **mammal** is a fierce **predator**. Another animal will make a tasty meal.

The mongoose senses movement in the grass. He spies a long, dark shape. The mongoose has come upon its **prey**: a king cobra. But the snake doesn't like that idea. The battle is about to begin!

The mongoose rushes toward the snake. He bites the snake with his sharp teeth. The king cobra rises up. She is ready to strike.

The cobra's head snaps quickly toward the mongoose. Her bite is full of deadly **venom**. Her teeth sink into the mongoose's furry body. But the mongoose is not ready to give up. Who will win this deadly battle?

The Cute (but Fierce!) Mongoose

A mongoose is a small, furry animal with a long tail. It measures 14 to 17 inches (36 to 45 cm) long. It weighs five to eleven pounds (2.3 to 5 kg)—about the same as a small dog. Males are larger than females.

There are more than two dozen different species of mongoose. Most live in warm places in Africa and Asia.

Make Some Noise!

Mongooses are noisy animals. They often chatter and chirp to each other.

Mongooses are **carnivores**. They only eat meat. A mongoose has very small eyes and ears, but it is good at finding prey to eat. They use their great senses of smell and hearing to find food.

A mongoose will eat just about any animal. Its favorite foods are birds, **reptiles**, and other small mammals. Mongooses usually hunt by themselves, but sometimes a group will hunt together. They are fearless. Their sharp teeth and claws are deadly weapons.

Good Morning!

Mongooses are active during the day. At night, they sleep in underground **burrows** or in trees.

A mongoose has thick fur. This fur helps protect it from snake bites. But the mongoose has another interesting defense against snakes—a snake's venom does not affect it! One bite from a cobra doesn't bother a mongoose. It takes a lot of bites to **inject** enough venom to kill a mongoose.

Mongooses will attack cobras for many reasons. Sometimes they are hunting for food, and cobras make a tasty meal. Other times, they need to protect baby mongooses from snakes that like to eat them.

A Famous Mongoose

"Rikki-Tikki-Tavi" is a famous story by Rudyard Kipling. In the story, Rikki-Tikki-Tavi is a mongoose that protects an English family from a pair of dangerous cobras.

A Deadly Snake

Cobras are the largest—and one of the most dangerous!—venomous snakes in the world.

Cobras are 6 feet long (1.8 meters) and weigh 4 to 10 pounds (1.8 to 4.5 kg). A king cobra, the largest species of cobra, can be up to 18 feet (5.6 meters) long! That's about the same as three refrigerators stacked on top of each other. They weigh 13 pounds (5.9 kg) or more.

Cobras are usually yellow, brown, green, or black. They have yellow or white markings on their bodies. Their bodies are covered with thick **scales** that protect them from predators.

King of Snakes

King cobras got their name because they are big enough to kill other cobras.

Cobras have many sharp senses. They have good eyesight. They also have a great sense of hearing. A cobra can hear the **vibrations** of an animal as it comes close.

A cobra's best sense is its sense of smell. Its forked tongue flicks in and out of its mouth to gather smells.

When a cobra attacks, it raises its head and spreads its neck to look bigger and more powerful. The snake may also puff or hiss. It lifts its body up tall. Then, the snake lunges forward. It sinks its long **fangs** into its prey.

A cobra's fangs are attached to **glands** in its jaws. These glands are full of venom. When a cobra bites, venom flows into the wound. A cobra's venom is strong enough to kill an elephant!

What's on the Menu?

Many cobras will eat birds, fish, frogs, and small mammals. But a king cobra's favorite food is other snakes. They rarely eat mammals or birds.

King cobras live in hot places in India and other parts of Asia. These snakes usually live alone. But males and females live together during mating season, which is about four months each year.

A male cobra needs to work hard to get a female's attention. Male cobras often fight to win a female mate. The males wrestle each other with their big bodies. The first snake to push the other snake's head to the ground wins.

A female cobra lays between 20 and 40 eggs. She piles leaves around the eggs and lies on top to keep the eggs warm. The male stays nearby to scare away any predators that might eat the eggs.

A Fight to the Death

Let's get back to the battle between the mongoose and the king cobra. The last time we saw them, the cobra had bitten the mongoose. But the mongoose has not backed down. These enemies are still fighting.

The cobra raises her body again. Her fangs sink into the mongoose's thick fur. Most of the bites don't reach the mongoose's skin. But some of them do.

Meanwhile, the mongoose keeps rushing at the snake. He bites the reptile. The mongoose's sharp teeth slash through the snake's thick scales.

The snake's venom is starting to affect the mongoose. He stumbles. But he is still not ready to give up. The mongoose bites the cobra again.

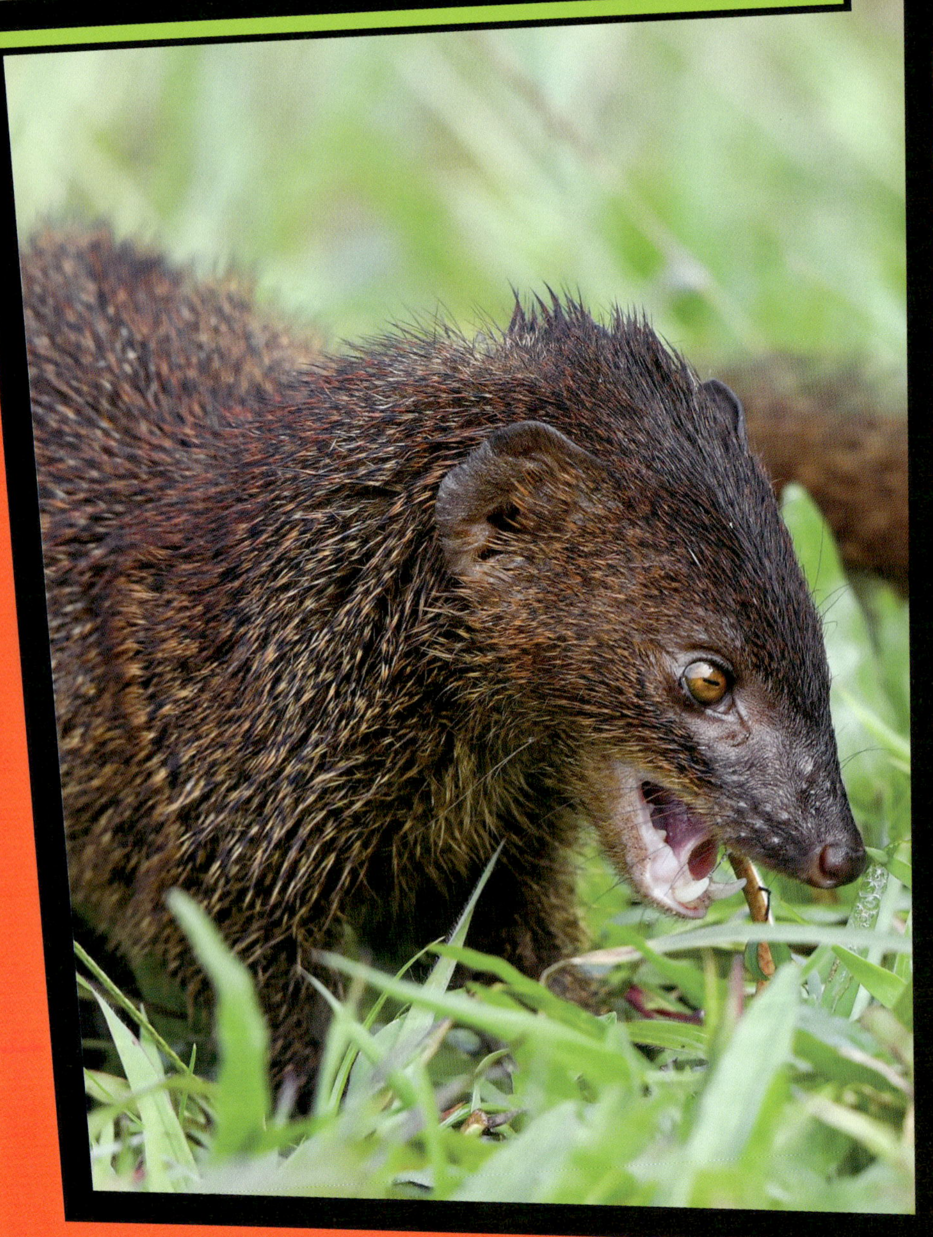

Blood seeps from the snake's scales. The snake drops to the ground. Will she slither away? No! She raises her head. She puffs out her neck. Then, this killer snake moves to strike the mongoose again.

How will this battle end? If the cobra bites the mongoose hard enough, its venom will kill the furry animal. But the mongoose's bite is strong enough to crush the cobra's head if it dares to get that close.

What will happen next? Think about each animal's weapons and defenses. Then, you decide! Who do you think will win this deadly battle?

Mongoose vs. Cobra

Range of Mongoose

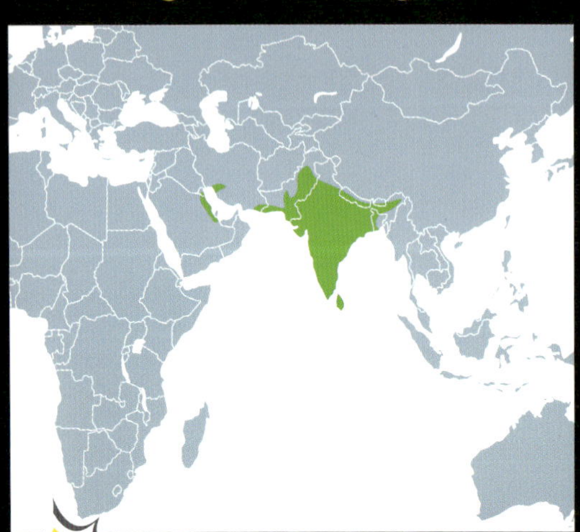

Range of Cobra

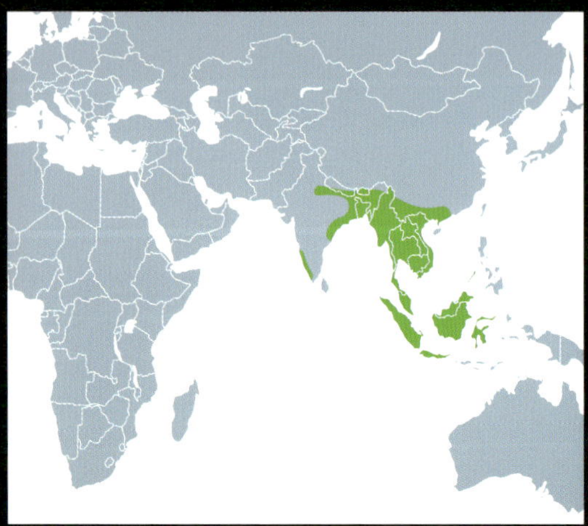

Mongoose: Weight—5 to 11 pounds (2.3 to 5 kg); Length—14 to 17 inches (36 to 45 cm)

Cobra: Weight—up to 13 pounds (5.9 kg) or more; Length—6 to 18 feet (1.8 to 5.6 meters)

Mongoose: 28 teeth, including four strong teeth that can break bones

Cobra: Two long fangs that deliver venom

Mongoose: Sharp claws, strong teeth, fast runner

Cobra: Venomous bite, moves fast

Mongoose: Resistant to venom, thick fur

Cobra: Thick scales, threatening behavior, large size

Glossary

burrows (BUR-ohz)
underground holes and tunnels where animals live

carnivores (KAHR-nuh-vorz)
animals that eat meat

fangs (FANGZ)
long, pointed teeth

glands (GLANDZ)
organs in the body that produce chemicals

inject (in-JEKT)
to force a liquid into the body

mammal (MAM-uhl)
an animal that is warm-blooded, has hair, and nurses its babies

predator (PRED-uh-tur)
an animal that hunts and eats other animals

prey (PRAY)
an animal hunted and eaten by another animal

reptiles (REP-tilez)
animals that are cold-blooded, have scales, and lay eggs

scales (SKALEZ)
thin, flat, overlapping pieces of skin that cover the body of a reptile

venom (VEN-uhm)
poison

vibrations (vye-BRAY-shuhnz)
rapid movements back and forth

Fact Check

1. A cobra's bite is full of ________ venom.
   A. harmless B. deadly C. tasty

2. Mongooses live in ________ places.
   A. wet B. warm C. dry

3. King cobras mostly eat ________.
   A. snakes B. mongooses C. mammals

4. A mongoose is not affected by a cobra's ________.
   A. fangs B. scales C. venom

Answers
1. B, 2. B, 3. A, 4. C

Further Reading

BOOKS

Aronson, Deb. *King Cobras*. Apex, 2024.

Boutland, Craig. *King Cobra*. Bearport Publishing, 2021.

Downs, Kieran. *King Cobra vs. Mongoose*. Bellwether Media, 2021.

ON THE INTERNET

Britannica Kids: Mongoose
kids.britannica.com/kids/article/mongoose/353484
This article includes interesting facts about mongooses, including where they live, what they eat, and how they hunt.

8 Magnificent Facts About Mongooses
www.treehugger.com/mongoose-facts-5075176
Check out this article for facts, photos, and a fun cartoon about mongooses.

National Geographic Kids: King Cobra
kids.nationalgeographic.com/animals/reptiles/facts/king-cobra
Learn all about the mighty king cobra.

About the Author

Joanne Mattern has written many nonfiction books for children. She adores animals of all kinds. Although she loves snakes, she's had a special place in her heart for mongooses ever since she read "Rikki-Tikki-Tavi" as a child. Joanne lives in New York State with her family, where there are poisonous snakes, but no cobras.